EXPLORING FILE I/O IN C

Codenewbie Programming

BY

JEFFREY DAHMER

COPYRIGHT

Table of Contents

INTRODUCTION

The ability to interact with data stored on our computers is enabled via file management, which is a basic part of programming. Mastering Input/Output (IO) operations is vital for every developer, whether it's reading text from a file, writing data to it, or modifying its contents.

This article will go through various file handling principles in C, such as low-level and high-level File I/O, file descriptors, and more.

The Importance of File Management

When a program is ended, all data is erased. Data will be saved in a file even if the application is terminated.

It will take some time to input a big amount of data. However, if you have a file that has all of the data, you can quickly retrieve it with a few instructions.

Handling of files The ability to read and write configuration files allows users to modify program settings to their tastes.

Programs that need to exchange data with other programs or systems may transfer data in different forms with other entities via file handling.

Saving data to files on a regular basis guarantees that important information may be recovered in the event of a system failure or data loss.

HOW TO BEGIN WITH FILE HANDLING

At its most basic, file handling is executing actions on files such as opening, reading, writing, and shutting them. File management in C programming is accomplished using the following methods:

Streams, file pointers, and file descriptors are all types of streams.

Let's take a closer look at them.

Streams

These are the core abstractions in C for file handling. They give a high-level reading and writing interface. files. In C, standard streams such as stdin (standard input), stdout (standard output), and stderr (standard error) are provided for input and output.

Pointers to Files

A file pointer is a technique that keeps track of a file's present location. It determines the location of the next read or write operation. File pointers are required for sequential file access and aid in navigating the file's contents.

Descriptors for Files

In C, these are low-level integer IDs for open files. As we discovered previously, each descriptor relates to a certain stream.

The table below summarizes the different descriptors and their associated streams.

INTEGER VALUE	NAME	SYMBOLIC CONSTANT	FILE STREAM

1	Standard Input	STDIN_FILENO	stdin
2	Standard Output	STDOUT_FILENO	stdout
3	Standard Error	STDERR_FILENO	stderr

NOTE

stdin: This variable is used to read input from the user or from another program.

stdout: This variable is used to send output to the user or another application.

Stderr is used to output error messages and other diagnostics to the user.

BASIC FILE HANDLING OPERATIONS IN C

In file management using C, there are four (4) basic operations. They are starting, reading, writing, and finishing. When managing and altering files, these steps must be done in the correct order.

Aside from the four (4) fundamental operations, there are normally two (2) techniques to dealing with them. There are two approaches: low-level using system calls and high-level with a standard library.

Another thing to keep in mind is that files come in a variety of forms, including csv, binary, and text. This essay will concentrate on Only the text files.

Let's go through the fundamentals of file management. We would examine each operation's implementation from both the high-level and low-level perspectives.

OPENING A DOCUMENT

This is the initial stage in managing files. It creates a link between your software and the file on disk.

The following parameters are specified during file opening.

The file's name, the location, and the mode in which you wish to open the file. These modes indicate what you want to do with the file you're opening. Reading just, writing only, adding, and so forth. Man fopening

High-Level Strategy

FILE = fopen("example.txt", "r");

RETURN VALUE: If successful, a FILE reference; else, NULL.

Low-Level Approach man open int fd = open("example.txt", O_RDONLY);

NEW RETURN VALUE: If successful, a file descriptor is returned; otherwise, -1 is returned.

Below explains several modes and how they correspond to one another in high-level and low-level methods.

mode fopen()open() parametersUsage

r r O_RDONLYFile is opened for reading.

O_RDWR r+File is opened for reading and writing.

O_WRONLY | O_CREATIVITY | O_TRUNCCreates a file. If there is existing text, it clears (truncates) everything w+ O_RDWR | O_CREAT | O_TRUNCIt is now possible to read and write. If the file does not exist, it is created; otherwise, it is truncated.

aO_WRONLY | O_CREATIVE | O_ADDAppending (writing at the end of the file) is enabled. If the file does not already exist, it is created.

READING DATA FROM A FILE

This entails reading data from an existing file on disk.

You may read data line by line or character by character. Depending on your program's requirements, you can do it line by line or in bigger chunks.

High-Level Strategy

With this strategy, there are two ways to read from files. They are as follows:

fgets() reads text line by line and saves it in a buffer.

while(fgets(buffer, sizeof(buffer), file)!= NULL) FILE *file; char buffer[1024]; // Go through each line of the file

RETURN VALUE: A string if successful, NULL if unsuccessful.

man fgets fread(): This function reads a given number of bytes from a file or, for binary files, into a buffer.

man frightened

```
FILE *file; char buffer[1024]; size_t
bytes_to_read = sizeof(buffer); size_t
bytes_to_read = fread(buffer, 1, bytes_to_read,
file); size_t bytes_to_read = fread(buffer, 1,
bytes_to_read, file);
```

VALUE RETURNED: The number of objects read

Low-Level Strategy

This makes use of the read() method.

```
read(fd, buffer, sizeof(buffer)); char
buffer[1024]; ssize_t bytes_read = read(fd,
buffer, sizeof(buffer));
```

If (bytes_read == -1), then

```
// handle the error; else, process the
information in the buffer
```

NOTE: The fd is the open function man read's return value.

CREATING A FILE

This inserts or modifies information in a file.

You have the option of writing character by character, line by line, or in bigger chunks.

Writing is required for operations such as writing log files, preserving program output, and archiving user-generated material.

High-Level Strategy

This approach use the fprintf() function (Write formatted text data to a file).

FILE *file = fopen("example.txt", "w"); // Open for writing fprintf(file, "Hello,%s!n", "World"); man fprintf fwrite()

*file = fopen("data.bin", "wb"); // Ready for binary writing

size_t bytes_to_write = sizeof(data); size_t bytes_written = fwrite(data, 1, bytes_to_write, file); man fwrite

Low-Level Strategy

The method used here is write().

```
const char *text = "Hello, World!"n; int fd =
open("example.txt", O_CREAT | O_WRONLY |
O_TRUNC, 0644); const char *text = "Hello,
World!"n; ssize_t bytes_tman write = write(fd,
text, strlen(text));
```

NOTE: Change the different modes/flags of the write operation to get the desired outcomes, such as add.

The low-level technique gives you more control over the writing process and allows you to directly edit the binary data. If you're working with text files, you must manage buffering and text encoding yourself.

This is the final stage in the file handling process, and it is critical for freeing up system resources and ensuring data integrity.

When you have finished reading or writing, you should close the file to free up the file descriptors and verify that any outstanding modifications have been completed. are preserved.

Failure to close a file property might result in data corruption and resource leakage.

High-level strategy

*file = fopen("example.txt", "w") // Open for writing // Write data to the file fclose(file); // When finished man fclose

Integer fd = open("example.txt", O_CREAT | O_WRONLY | O_TRUNC, 0644); // Open for writing // Write data to the file close(fd); // When finished, shut the file descriptor man close

You may have noticed that there are two techniques to handline files in C. The high-level technique is the most commonly utilized. However, let us examine some distinctions between the two. This would let us decide which of them to utilize at what point in time.

ASPECTHIGH-LEVEL STRATEGYLOW-LEVEL STRATEGY

The representation of a fileFor file operations, a file stream represented by *FILE** is used.For file operations, *int* file descriptors are used.

Common dutiesFopen(), fclose(), fgets(), fprintf(), and fwrite() are all common functions.Open(), close(), read(), and write() are all common functions.

Binary vs. Text FilesSuitable for both text and binary files, with text encoding and formatting features.Suitable for both text and binary files, however text encoding and formatting must be handled manually if necessary.

Error Handling Errors are handled using routines such as ferror() and feof().Error handling is based on error codes supplied by methods such as read() and write().

Cleanup of ResourcesWhen you use fclose(), it automatically flushes data and releases resources.For resource cleaning, file descriptors must be manually closed using close().

Let us now go on.

PRACTICAL QUESTIONS

QUESTION 1

Implement a program to read text from a file

SOLUTION

High level approach

```c
#include <stdio.h>
#include <stdlib.h>

int main(int argc, char *argv[]) {
    if (argc != 2) {
        printf("Usage: %s source_file\n", argv[0]);
        return 1;
    }

    FILE *source = fopen(argv[1], "r");

    if (!source) {
```

```c
        perror("Error");
        return 1;
    }

    char buffer[1024];

    while (fgets(buffer, sizeof(buffer), source)) {
        printf("%s", buffer);
    }

    fclose(source);

    return 0;
}
```

Low level approach

```c
#include <stdio.h>
```

```c
#include <stdlib.h>
#include <unistd.h>
#include <fcntl.h>

int main(int argc, char *argv[]) {
    if (argc != 2) {
        printf("Usage: %s source_file\n", argv[0]);
        return 1;
    }

    int source_fd = open(argv[1], O_RDONLY);

    if (source_fd == -1) {
        perror("Error");
        return 1;
    }
```

```c
    char buffer[1024];

    ssize_t bytes_read;


    while ((bytes_read = read(source_fd, buffer,
sizeof(buffer))) > 0) {

        if (write(STDOUT_FILENO, buffer,
bytes_read) == -1) {

            perror("Error");

            return 1;

        }

    }


    close(source_fd);


    return 0;
```

```
}
```

QUESTION 2

Implement a program to append some text to a file. This program should take the text from the user (stdin) and then append to the file

SOLUTION

High level approach

```c
#include <stdio.h>

#include <stdlib.h>


int main(int argc, char *argv[]) {
    if (argc != 2) {
        printf("Usage:    %s    destination_file\n", argv[0]);
        return 1;
```

```c
    }

    FILE *destination = fopen(argv[1], "a");

    if (!destination) {
        perror("Error");
        return 1;
    }

    char input[1024];

    printf("Enter text (Ctrl-D to end):\n");

    while (fgets(input, sizeof(input), stdin)) {
        fputs(input, destination);
    }
```

```c
    fclose(destination);

    return 0;
}
```

Low level approach

```c
#include <stdio.h>

#include <stdlib.h>

#include <unistd.h>

#include <fcntl.h>

int main(int argc, char *argv[]) {
    if (argc != 2) {

        printf("Usage: %s destination_file\n", argv[0]);

        return 1;
```

```c
    }


    int destination_fd = open(argv[1],
O_WRONLY | O_CREAT | O_APPEND,
0644);


    if (destination_fd == -1) {

        perror("Error");

        return 1;

    }


    char input[1024];


    printf("Enter text (Ctrl-D to end):\n");


    while (fgets(input, sizeof(input), stdin)) {
```

```c
    if (write(destination_fd, input, strlen(input)) == -1) {

        perror("Error");

        return 1;

        }

    }


    close(destination_fd);


    return 0;

}
```

QUESTION 3

Implement a File Copy Program (like cp command)

SOLUTION

High level approach

```c
#include <stdio.h>
#include <stdlib.h>

int main(int argc, char *argv[]) {
    if (argc != 3) {
        printf("Usage: %s source_file destination_file\n", argv[0]);
        return 1;
    }

    FILE *source = fopen(argv[1], "rb");
    FILE *destination = fopen(argv[2], "wb");

    if (!source || !destination) {
```

```c
        perror("Error");

        return 1;

    }


    char buffer[1024];

    size_t bytes_read;


    while ((bytes_read = fread(buffer, 1,
sizeof(buffer), source)) > 0) {

        fwrite(buffer, 1, bytes_read, destination);

    }


    fclose(source);

    fclose(destination);


    return 0;
```

```
}
```

Low level approach

```c
#include <stdio.h>

#include <stdlib.h>

#include <unistd.h>

#include <fcntl.h>


int main(int argc, char *argv[]) {
    if (argc != 3) {
        printf("Usage: %s source_file destination_file\n", argv[0]);
        return 1;
    }


    int source_fd = open(argv[1], O_RDONLY);
```

```c
    int destination_fd = open(argv[2],
O_WRONLY | O_CREAT | O_TRUNC, 0644);


    if (source_fd == -1 || destination_fd == -1) {

        perror("Error");

        return 1;

    }


    char buffer[1024];

    ssize_t bytes_read;


    while ((bytes_read = read(source_fd, buffer,
sizeof(buffer))) > 0) {

        if (write(destination_fd, buffer, bytes_read)
== -1) {

            perror("Error");

            return 1;
```

```
        }

    }


    close(source_fd);

    close(destination_fd);


    return 0;

}
```

NOTE: The open() method contains an optional input called as permissions in low-level implementation. The file permissions that you may configure are read, write, and execute, which are represented by numerical numbers.